This book is dedicated to Sarai, Frenchaire-Two,
Melchizedek Malcolm X, Joseph Jr.
and my mama Virgie Gardner.
I love you.

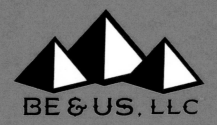

BE & US, LLC

bytesize.me/beandusllc

Mommy & Daddy, Do You Still Love Me Anymore?

Written By
Frenchaire Gardner

Our family was always
together happily.
We had so much fun.
We ran around in the yard
and sang songs in the street.

People would approach us with their arms stretched out wide, offering caresses, candy, or even clothes.

They called us "Indigo" kids.

One thing is for sure--our family did things our own way. One of us was even born on the city bus. I guess Melchizedek just couldn't wait to join our family. His birth announcement even made the newspaper!

No matter what, our family always stuck together. First, it was just us three-- Mommy, Daddy, and me. Then came my sister Frenchaire-Two, my brother Melchizedek and finally baby Sarai.

Daddy always cooked our meals and you played with us. There was always something to do--reading lots of books, practicing words and our ABCs, and learning our numbers.

If love were money, we would have been millionaires. Mommy worried a lot about money.

Sometimes we didn't have gas, lights, or even water in our house. When that happened, we'd barbeque outside. We'd go on scavenger hunts and find places to fill up water jugs so we could drink, cook, and stay clean.

Time flies when you're having fun--
especially tough times. We had a blast
gathering wood and twigs to light and
build fires for Daddy to use for cooking
breakfast, lunch or dinner. We'd all
gather around, laughing and singing.
Mama called it camping.

When things got really tough,
Mommy would ask people for money
so we could eat, or so she could buy
diapers and pay for a day in a hotel.

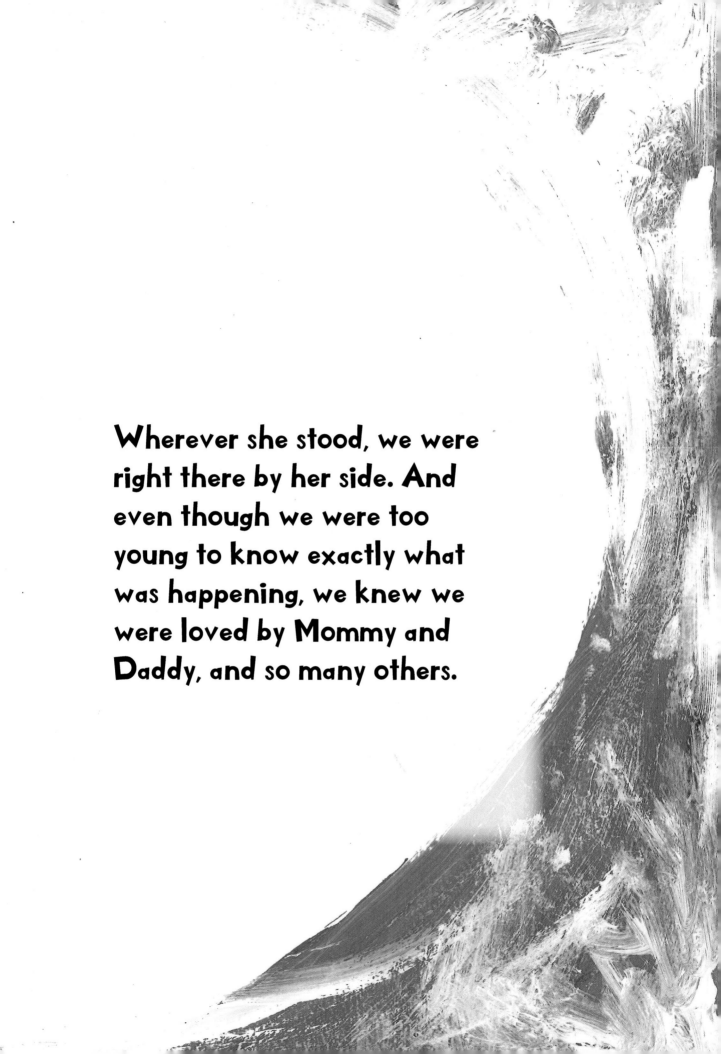

Wherever she stood, we were right there by her side. And even though we were too young to know exactly what was happening, we knew we were loved by Mommy and Daddy, and so many others.

Even though they told us kids not to argue and fight, Mommy and Daddy did...all the time.

They argued way too much,
so much that we'd get
scared that someone would
get hurt or taken away to
adult time-out--jail.

But when Mommy and Daddy were working, things were better and the days seemed much brighter. We'd shop for new clothes and have special treats.

Then hard times would hit again, and we'd be back in long lines. Some of them seemed like they'd never end! There were lines to eat, lines to just pick up food, and lines for clothes.

We'd count people and play games to pass the time.

No matter the situation, Mommy and Daddy made every day an adventure.

We'd jam to tunes playing on the radio that was attached to baby Sarai's stroller. It was so much fun.

Even though adults tell kids not to fuss and fight, sometimes they do it themselves. And that was the case with Mommy and Daddy--even though nobody liked it when it happened. Sometimes, when the arguments were too long or loud, Mommy or Daddy had to go to something like adult time-out, a place called jail.

Mommy told us to always go where the love is, so that's what we did.
We moved.
We had each other, and our new puppy.

We didn't see **Daddy** so much around
that time, but we saw plenty of
Grandma and **Grandpa**, who would
watch us while **Mommy** worked.

We had our new routine down pat--
First breakfast, then brushing our teeth and getting
dressed, then it was off to school while Mommy worked,
then she'd pick us up from school and we'd catch the
bus home. One day, while on our way to see the doctor,
Daddy showed up at the bus stop. We were so excited to
see him! It had been so long.

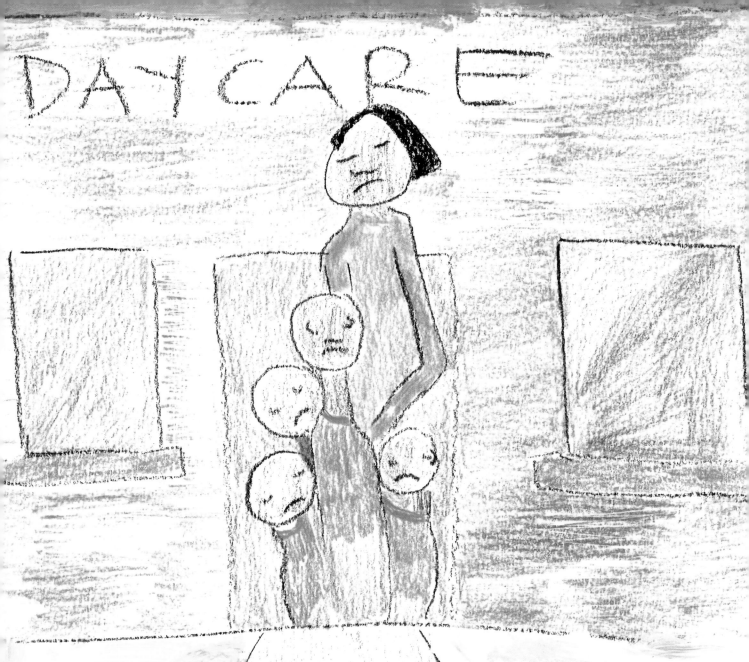

Because Mommy and Daddy argued so much, a judge gave them lots of rules to follow for themselves, and for us. One rule was that we weren't supposed to see our father. There were people called social workers who checked up on our family to make sure we were alright and that our parents were following the rules. After the social worker found out we'd seen our dad, the biggest change of all came.

One afternoon, the social worker picked all four of us up from daycare instead of Mommy.

From then on, we stayed in different homes with people who wanted to care for us. Some were really kind, others not so much.

We still kept in touch with Mommy the whole time and spoke to her on the computer once a week. She'd asked us all about the interesting stuff--how we were doing, what we learned in school, and our friends' names. We mostly asked about our Daddy.

Eventually, different foster homes became just one. Mommy was the one to tell us that someone in another state had adopted us, and we would be starting a brand new life. We all felt so much-- too much to put into words.

Mommy assured us, "Time
and space cannot separate us.
We are one. I am you
and you are me. And I love
you, no matter where you are."

That was seven years ago. We're all growing and changing and learning so much at school. Sometimes, when things are quiet, we all wonder, "Mommy and Daddy, do you all love us still?"

And even though she's not right next to us every single day, we can feel Mommy's words echo in our hearts:

"Time and space cannot separate us. We are one. I am you and you are me. And I love you, no matter where you are."

Made in the USA
Coppell, TX
30 May 2023

17478772R00024